Diminishing Resources: Oil

Timothy Gardner
AR B.L.: 9.1 Alt.: 1350
Points: 3.0                    MG

# Diminishing Resources
# Oil

# Diminishing Resources
# Oil

Timothy Gardner

MORGAN
REYNOLDS
PUBLISHING

Greensboro, North Carolina

# Diminishing Resources
## SERIES

# Soil | Forests | Water | Oil

# Diminishing Resources: Oil

Copyright © 2010 by Morgan Reynolds Publishing

Library of Congress Cataloging-in-Publication Data

Gardner, Timothy, 1966-
       Diminishing Resources: Oil / by Timothy Gardner. – 1st ed.
              p.   cm.
       Includes bibliographical references and index.
       ISBN 978-1-59935-117-9 (alk. paper)
   1.      Petroleum—Juvenile literature. 2.  Petroleum—United
           States—History—Juvenile literature. 3.  Petroleum
           industry and trade—Juvenile literature. 4.  Petroleum
           industry and trade—United States—History—Juvenile
           literature. 5.  Petroleum conservation—United States—
           Juvenile literature.  I. Title.  II. Title: Oil.
       TN870.3.G37 2009
       333.8'232—dc22

                                                        2009010245

Printed in the United States of America
First Edition

*To two teachers, Nancy and Lloyd*

# Contents

# Chapter One
## The Gathering Storms

The news from Thunder Horse—one of the world's largest oil platforms, 150 miles out in the deep green waters of the Gulf of Mexico—in early July 2005 was not good. Workers sailing back to the platform after Hurricane Dennis discovered it had been knocked over. The platform looked like a giant table with one end dipping into the ocean. British Petroleum (BP) had expected to open the $1 billion structure in weeks. Now oil output was delayed indefinitely. "Hurricane season is one of the realities of operating in the gulf," said a BP spokeswoman.

The platform, designed to drill five miles down through ocean and rock, represented the new oil frontier. After nearly 150 years of drilling on the mainland, U.S. oil was harder to find. So companies invested heavily in ultra-deep offshore drilling, despite the prevalent threats of hurricane season.

A month after Dennis, Hurricane Katrina ripped through the gulf toppling more platforms and rigs. In September, Hurricane Rita wiped out still more. The deadly storms ground Gulf oil output nearly to a halt for months, sent overall U.S. crude production to the lowest level since World War II, and punished drivers the world over with high gasoline prices. Thunder Horse only began limited production three years later.

The hurricanes were a lesson to many Americans that drillers were pumping a quarter of the country's domestic oil from high-risk areas. But vulnerability to hurricanes was just one symptom of the addiction of the world's top energy consumer. Indeed, the United States imports about 65 percent of its crude oil from abroad—often from countries the government does not consider friendly.

The U.S. military spends taxpayer money protecting oil delivery, whether it's for shipping lanes for tankers from the Middle East or a pipeline in Colombia. That's because modern America was built on a supply of cheap oil. Cars, buses, trucks, ships, trains, and airplanes all burn oil products. Roads are made of asphalt, the stuff from the bottom of the oil barrel.

Our food system depends on fossil fuels, whether it's fertilizer which is made with natural gas, or the energy it took to deliver food from the farm to the plate. Plastic, which is mostly made from oil, keeps food from rotting, provides much of the equipment in hospitals, and helped launch the computer age with hardware frames, printers, and keyboards. Cheap oil has even shaped where Americans live, allowing millions to live in the suburbs and commute to work.

Thunder Horse, the largest oil producer in the Gulf of Mexico, on July 12, 2005, after Hurricane Dennis.

Americans began to wonder what life after cheap oil looked like when rising global demand helped push oil prices to $147 per barrel in the summer of 2008, contributing to the worst economic crisis since the Great Depression. Drivers balked at the high prices and cut down on driving, which helped knock more than $100 a barrel off oil. But once the economy improves, analysts expect oil prices to head up.

Nobody knows how long relatively cheap oil will last, and the best experts can do is make an educated guess. The International Energy Agency, an advisor to twenty-seven industrialized countries, said in its 2008 outlook that global oil production should not peak before 2030. In 2008, the world burned about 85 million barrels per day (bpd) and that should rise to 106 million bpd in 2030, based on increased demand from China, India, and the Middle East.

One thing is certain, though. Drillers will look to riskier frontiers—even to the ends of the Earth—for new oil sources. Things have changed since the days when oil was so plentiful some considered it a nuisance.

# Chapter Two
# Pennsylvania Hills

S amuel Kier almost quit the western Pennsylvania salt drilling business in 1847 because his derricks were pulling up green goo along with the brine. He let the oil float to the top of his salt-water boilers and then dumped it into a canal that led into the Allegheny River. Then one day boys playing with matches lit the canal on fire and nearly burned down the surrounding houses.

A year later Kier's wife, Nancy, fell ill and a doctor recommended she take a local cure called rock oil. She seemed to improve, so Kier examined it, determining it was similar to the stuff in his brine. Kier trained salesmen to peddle bottles of "Kiers' Petroleum or American Rock Oil" from horse-drawn wagons. The showy salesmen hit the northeast claiming the patent medicine could ease everything from constipation to skin problems. Kier began selling it directly to druggists. He had no way of knowing that would help a well-connected New York lawyer to spark a chain of events bringing about the American oil business that helped the country become the world's industrial giant.

Natives in western Pennsylvania knew about oil long before Kier did. The Senecas had applied it to wounds and burned it in ceremonies for hundreds of years. It bubbled up from the ground in pools along a tributary of the Allegheny that Europeans dubbed Oil Creek.

In the East, oil had been known since ancient times. Hit, not far from modern Baghdad, was a source of oil since 3000

BC. Builders used thick oil for mortar in the city walls of Jericho and Babylon, shipbuilders waterproofed boats with it, and workers built roads with the asphalt. It was also used as a tool of war. The Byzantines attacked ships with burning oil bombs and shot flaming arrows that had been dipped in oil. Workers in China drilled oil from below the ground with bamboo pipes, but its early petroleum pioneers didn't find crude in large quantities.

One day in 1856, George Bissell, the New York lawyer, saw an advertisement for Kier's Petroleum in the window of a pharmacy. Bissell had been trying to convince his business partners oil could be a huge money-maker if they sold it as an illuminant for lamps around the globe. Oil could also lubricate the nation's growing machinery fleet. But nobody knew how to suck it up from underground. Bissell wondered if the salt-water drilling derricks pictured in Kier's poster were the answer.

At that time, oil extracted from whales was the main illuminant burned in lamps. At first, workers simply butchered whales that had beached on the shores of New England and melted the blubber into oil. Not enough came from that source, so they hunted whales from boats. Soon crews had to go out thousands of miles, turning eventually to the Pacific. As a result, the price of whale oil surged to several dollars a

Samuel Kier

In the early days of the oil industry, derricks were often built close together to get as much oil out of the ground as possible. *(Library of Congress)*

gallon, making it a fuel for the rich. Regular people resorted to burning smelly pig lard or sooty fuel made from coal.

Bissell's partners chose "Colonel" E. Drake to direct well drilling in Titusville, near Oil Creek. He designed a derrick to smash a metal shaft through rock. In 1859, his team struck oil. The locals, who had previously thought Drake was crazy, ransacked homes and barns for buckets and bins and bathtubs—anything to contain the crude.

News of Drake's strike drew workers from all corners of the country, who soon built a forest of derricks. Boomtowns shot up complete with luxury hotels. The quiet hills of western Pennsylvania had never heard such a din.

Fortunes were made and the oil lit up the night for millions of people. But it was not all good news. One of the first wells caught fire, killing nineteen people. Oil prices tanked as supply outstripped demand and then rose rapidly again, making lucky

An 1891 print compares the first oil well drilled by "Colonel" Edwin Drake in 1859 to a "modern" oil well. *(Library of Congress)*

**The First Oil Well.**

Drilled by Col. Drake in 1859, near Titusville, Pa.

the Oil Well Supply Co.

**1859.**

**THE OLD** an

THE FIRST OIL WELL, HEIGHT OF DERRICK 34 FEET.

Both Derricks Draw

Col. E. L. Drake.

d THE NEW. 1891.

MODERN OIL WELL, HEIGHT OF DERRICK, 82 FEET.

wn to the same Scale.

Compliments of

OIL WELL SUPPLY COMPANY,

Pittsburgh, Bradford and Oil City, Pa.

New York City.

investors rich, and devastating others. Oil rings, or groups hoping to control prices by buying up supplies, began to form and then crumbled when prices fell unexpectedly. Towns died almost overnight when wells ran dry. Teamsters carrying the crude away in horse carts turned lanes into slick rivers of oil and mud, and horses that slipped and broke their legs were left to rot.

Drillers poked holes in the ground as fast as they could. In the rush, the natural gas associated with oil that helped push crude to the surface—much like carbon dioxide gas in shaken soda pushes drink out after the lid is cracked—escaped, keeping much of the oil out of reach underground.

Workers began to lay down oil's delivery system. Entrepreneurs built wooden pipelines that carried crude from wells to railroads, shocking people who didn't believe oil could be pumped uphill. Railroads built special cars to carry crude. Watercrafts hauling oil and equipment clogged the Allegheny.

The United States dominated the early global oil business, partially because its supplies were closer to markets than oil being developed in places like Baku, near the Caspian Sea. Companies grew with little government regulation. And of course, there were entrepreneurs, like John D. Rockefeller, an Ohio bookkeeper, who built the model for the modern oil company, becoming one of history's richest men.

Rockefeller sank his $700 savings into refineries. He cut costs at every opportunity, helping him gain control of the industry. Rockefeller bought tracks of Ohio forest, for example, to supply wood for the barrels, and made the wood lighter by drying it in kilns to reduce transport costs.

Soon cities around the world yearned for cheap American oil, but sailors didn't ship it because they were afraid the cargo would catch fire. In 1861, a Philadelphia shipper got a crew drunk and tricked them to aboard his oil ship. The shipment reached London safely, opening up the export business. The lamp fuel was especially popular in Russia where northern cities like St. Petersburg enjoyed only a few hours of sunlight during the winter. The availability of American oil pushed Russia to drill its own oil reservoirs, especially around the Caspian Sea, but growth was slow because there was only one refinery.

Rockefeller found uses for the entire barrel of oil, which could be refined into several products, including lamp fuel, machine lubrication oil, and the motor fuels diesel and gasoline. He ploughed profits right back into oil. "Take out what you've got to have to live on, but leave the rest in," he told his partners. "Don't buy new clothes and fast horses; let your wife wear her last year's bonnet. You can't find any place where money will earn what it does here." When there was no more equipment to buy he kept large reserves of cash. The money served as protection because nobody was sure when the oil would run out. And if new oil supplies were found, companies with cash could get to it first.

Rockefeller founded Standard Oil in 1870, and it quickly became the world's largest company. But the industry was plagued by ups and downs as oil towns boomed and busted, with refineries always either starved or glutted with crude.

Oil baron John D. Rockefeller

There was also growing competition for global oil markets. In Baku, which is now part of Azerbaijan, oilmen were striking wells that flowed like fountains called gushers. The oil was more than Russia could use, so producers exported it, taking market share from the United States.

Rockefeller controlled his company even more tightly and Standard became a virtual monopoly. He brought together the two ends of the industry—drilling for oil and refining—under one company to eliminate price swings. In addition he bought many refineries run by other companies. They didn't have much choice. If a company didn't want to sell, he'd simply lower fuel prices until it had no chance of surviving. Rockefeller soon controlled 90 percent of all oil refined in the United States.

Twenty years after Drake hit oil, an event threatened the petroleum business. Thomas Alva Edison invented the light bulb in 1879 and built a giant power-generating station in Manhattan—fueled by coal, not oil. European cities took to electric lights as well. But soon, the development of cars, which ran on oil-fueled combustion engines, created a thirst for oil that dwarfed that for lamps and changed the lives of millions. Cars brought new riches to Rockefeller and other oilmen. Skeptics derided the early "horseless carriages," because they were slower, noisier, and more dependent than horse-pulled carts. The San Francisco earthquake of 1906 changed many minds, however, when rescuers commandeered automobiles off sales lots to help save victims.

In 1908, Henry Ford announced mass production of the Model T car, the embodiment of his dream to create an affordable, durable car for the masses. Cars soon enabled a way of life and a philosophy for Americans that the open road was a path to freedom. "Every day is 'Independence Day' to him who owns a Ford," one advertisement declared in 1913.

More sources of crude had been found in California, Oklahoma, and especially Texas. America's first gusher came from a hill called Spindletop in Texas. Initial flow from the first well was more than all wells in the United States combined.

Workers flocked to nearby Beaumont. Lucky ones slept in tents or took turns resting in the few beds. Others slept in the street. Overcrowding and an abundance of alcohol at the saloons led to violence—there were fights and murders nearly every Saturday night.

Major U.S. oil companies—such as Texaco and Gulf—took root. The potential for riches also attracted foreigners like Marcus Samuel, a London shipper who had once worked in his father's shop selling shell-covered boxes. He had built tankers to take oil from Russia to Singapore and Bangkok for his company Shell Transport and Trading, a precursor to Shell Oil, and was eager to get a piece of the action. He signed a deal with a Texas driller to transport the oil to international customers attempting to protect his company from Standard's global dominance. Standard was already supplying much of the lamp fuel for Chinese cities.

International oil companies weren't the only ones worried about Standard's influence in the oil market. Unions and politicians had tried to air Rockefeller's ruthless practices for years. Rockefeller met his rival in the journalist Ida Tarbell, who grew up in Pennsylvania oil country. She wrote a series in *McClure's Magazine* that ran from 1902 to 1904 exposing how Rockefeller broke independent oil companies by underselling them and controlling railroad fees. The series was full of admiration for his mind but also loaded with invective, calling Rockefeller "the oldest man in the world—a living mummy."

Tarbell's work inspired public outrage. In 1904, President Theodore Roosevelt launched an investigation into Standard Oil and two years later sued the company for conspiring to limit trade. The court ruled in Roosevelt's favor. Standard appealed, taking the case to the Supreme Court. Finally, in May 1911, the Supreme Court ordered Standard to be broken up. The company ultimately splintered into thirty separate ones. Two of the largest, Standard Oil of New Jersey, which eventually became Exxon, and Standard Oil of New York, which became Mobil, were stripped of their domestic crude supplies, leading them to seek new ones overseas.

Meanwhile, a flood of oil from Mexico and Venezuela helped push petroleum prices down. Petroleum became a convenient fuel for trains and ships, pushing demand even higher. New ways to distribute fuel also emerged. In 1907, entrepreneurs in St. Louis filled two hot water heaters with gasoline, attached hoses to them, and opened the first U.S. filling station. Oil had become a vital part of the American economy and way of life. Its influence was spreading, unstoppably, across the globe.

Old fashioned wooden oil derrick, Taft, Kern County, California.

# Chapter Three
# Ruling the Seas

Starting in the late 1890s, Germany and Britain, both industrial powerhouses, raced to build Europe's largest navy. Russia, France, and Austria-Hungary also bolstered their fleets. Winston Churchill, who had accepted the top civilian job for Britain's Royal Navy, set about getting the force in shape for war, should it be needed.

Churchill embraced the notion that switching the navy from coal to oil would make it more deadly than the German fleet. The government opposed such a move, reasoning that Britain could easily tap bountiful coal supplies in Wales, but it had virtually no oil supplies of its own. Britain would need foreign crude supplies, which in turn would require a military presence to keep flowing. If the fleet converted, it would be expensive to turn back.

Still, oil's advantages were many. Oil-fueled ships had greater acceleration and higher top speeds. Plus, more of the crew on an oil-powered ship could man guns rather than shovel coal. That could mean the difference between victory and defeat in a battle.

Meanwhile, the government of Persia (today Iran) needed money and offered investments in its bountiful oil supplies. The British supported William Knox D'Arcy, a capitalist given to horse racing, to negotiate with Persia and in 1901 he signed a deal. In exchange for 40,000 British pounds, worth about $5 million today, and a percentage of the profits, Persia would allow oil production for sixty years. It was the first "concession" in which western companies got the right to explore, produce, and own oil on sovereign lands. The first oil was struck in Persia in 1908.

Churchill decided in 1912 to change the Navy to oil. Britain then sought more control of the Middle East's top resource. He pushed Britain to take a 51 percent interest in the oil company Anglo-Persian, a precursor to British Petroleum (BP). Two years later, members of a Serbian nationalist group shot Archduke Franz Ferdinand, the heir to Austria-Hungary's throne, disrupting Europe's alliances and sparking World War I. Germany declared war on Russia and advanced into neutral countries, and Britain declared war on Germany.

The battles of World War I were unlike anything before. It was a mechanized war fought by land, sea, and sky. The British introduced the Little Willie, the first tank to run on gasoline, and soon there were thousands. Trucks, cars, and motorcycles joined battles, while airplanes fought in the sky and introduced bomb dropping to war.

All those engines drank fuel. World oil demand shot from 500,000 bpd in 1900 to 1.25 million bpd in 1915. The United States provided almost all of the oil for the Allies during the war. When German submarines attacked tankers filled with "Texas tea," as oil was sometimes called, it helped pull the United States into the war.

Geologists said even more Middle Eastern oil lay in Mosul, in what would eventually become Iraq. After the war, Britain and France carved Iraq from the former Turkish Empire, and companies partially owned by their governments split the oil wealth.

U.S. officials in Washington feared the British and French would dominate oil development in the Middle East. For one thing, if the Europeans flooded the global market with the region's crude, the least expensive in the world to produce, it would hurt America's oil producers in the Southwest and elsewhere. Washington also worried the Europeans threatened U.S. access to future Persian Gulf petroleum supplies.

Winston Churchill

Nobody was sure how long U.S. oil reserves would last. Even as the government imposed "gasoline-less Sundays" and other rations on motorists during the war, fuel demand rocketed as consumers bought new cars. The number of registered U.S. motor vehicles jumped from 1.8 to 9.2 million between 1914 and 1920. Under the circumstances, U.S. President Woodrow Wilson urged Britain to allow U.S. companies to drill in Iraq.

The Rockefeller "baby" companies had been looking for concessions in the Middle East since their domestic supplies had been cut off by the breakup of the parent company. The Standard Oil Company of New York persuaded the U.S. State Department to pressure the British to open development in the Middle East. Worried about a U.S. retaliation on British commerce, London in 1922 gave U.S. companies stakes in the European consortium called the Iraq Petroleum Company (IPC).

In 1928, the U.S. and European firms set up a pact to control oil production in the region. Under the "Red Line Agreement," they drew a line on a map around the old Turkish Empire from Turkey to Saudi Arabia, from the Suez Canal to Iran, and agreed not to drill there unless they had approval from the group. At a time of surging oil supply, the agreement effectively kept the companies' profits relatively high by limiting output from the region.

Meanwhile, other industrialized countries that had little oil at home looked outward for supply. Japan, for example, gained control of oilfields in Sumatra and Borneo. In the midst of World War II, Japan launched a surprise kamikaze attack on U.S. ships at Pearl Harbor in Hawaii in 1941 in part to prevent them from slowing its tankers going to the oil-rich East Indies. The attack pushed Washington to enter the war.

Germany had imperialistic goals, yet very little oil of its own. Adolf Hitler saw oil as the blood for Germany's rapid reindustrialization and militarization after it lost World War I. The country even entered the alternative fuels business by

taking over a company that had discovered how to make diesel fuel from coal, of which Germany had plenty. Germany
built a fleet of the synthetic fuel plants, and filled them with
workers taken from concentration camps. The Nazis also
advanced on Russia and North Africa in part to secure oilfields. Ironically, its tanks and trucks ran out of fuel, leading
to stinging defeats. And in 1944, American planes bombed
the synthetic fuel plants, contributing to Germany's defeat.

The battles of World War II made the United States
anxious to secure new oil. The U.S. petroleum admin-
istrator Harold Ickes had published a
paper entitled "We're
Running Out
of Oil!,"

warning President Franklin Roosevelt that if World War III broke out the country would not have enough. In 1943, Roosevelt authorized food, money, and equipment assistance to Saudi Arabia, which geologists said had more crude than Iran or Iraq.

Since 1915, Britain had protected the region known as Saudi Arabia. London thought the arrangement would secure its interests in the Middle East but also in its wider empire. After all, Arabia was home to the Islamic holy site of Mecca and under its colony of India, Britain ruled the largest number of Muslims in the world. Meanwhile the warrior Ibn Saud led battles against local tribes and in 1932 declared himself king of Saudi Arabia. It was the beginning of Britain's loss of control in the Middle East.

The battles had drained Ibn Saud of money, so to fund his fight for independence, he sold the one thing his country had much of: oil. In 1933, he granted Standard Oil of California (Socal) sixty-year concessions in exchange for a heap of gold. Socal brought in the Texas Oil Company to help pay for the costs of drilling in the punishing desert. They struck oil and formed the Arabian American Oil Company, or Aramco, in 1944. Today is the world's largest energy company, though Saudi Arabia has since taken it over.

On Valentine's Day 1945, President Roosevelt met the Saudi king on board the USS *Quincy*, near the Suez Canal. They got along well, despite their vast differences on the issue of Jewish immigration to Palestine, which the king opposed. Roosevelt, a smoker, refrained from lighting up in front of the king, who as a Muslim, opposed tobacco. Roosevelt, who suffered from polio, gave the king, whose war wounds made walking painful, a spare wheelchair. The king cherished the gift and the meeting marked the beginning of official relations between the world's top oil consumer and the country with the globe's biggest crude reservoirs.

Then the king let more American oil companies in, with Standard oil of New York (Exxon) and Standard oil of New

Opposite Page: The USS *West Virginia* went up in flames, after being hit by at least six torpedoes fired by the Japanese during the attack at Pearl Harbor. *(Courtesy of the Naval Historical Foundation)*

Jersey (Mobil) buying their way into Aramco. The U.S. multinational oil companies wanted to build a pipeline to bring the bounty of crude from sparsely populated Arabia to European cities where demand for cars and fuel was booming. Aramco completed the 1,100 mile Trans-Arabian Pipeline in 1950.

After the war, the United States lifted gasoline rations and car sales raced higher, with the number of registered U.S. passenger cars nearly doubling to 48 million. As demand rose in the late 1940s, the United States for the first time imported more oil than it produced.

Oilmen working for the largest western companies operating in the Middle East controlled petroleum prices with agreements between themselves. They also controlled the rate of investment in the region's oil business. Middle Eastern oil producing countries had few other exports of value so the energy companies in effect determined the economies and governmental budgets in the regions where they operated.

Meanwhile, people in oil-rich countries all over the world began demanding a larger share of oil profits. Vilification of foreign oil "invaders" was popular in Venezuelan novels and speeches, and in 1948, Venezuela forced the oil companies Royal Dutch Shell and Exxon to split profits with the government fifty-fifty.

King Ibn Saud kept one eye on Venezuela and the other on who made money on his kingdom's oil. He learned the taxes the U.S. government received from its oil companies working in Saudi Arabia were more than his own country took in total oil sales. The Saudis "weren't a darn bit happy about that," the American head of Aramco told the U.S. government. In 1950, the king forced the companies to accept a fifty-fifty split of Aramco's revenues.

In Iran, resentment against Britain's concession and colonialism had mounted for decades. Between 1945 and 1950, Anglo-Iranian Oil made about three times as much from Iranian oil as Iran itself made. Control of the country's riches by foreigners stirred angry crowds. The nationalist

Mohammed Mossadegh, the head of the oil committee in parliament, urged Iran to get more than half of the profits. When Prime Minister Ali Razmara came out against nationalization in March 1951 he was assassinated days later. Mossadegh, who replaced him, nationalized the industry and kicked British soldiers and businessmen out of the country.

In response, Washington pushed the U.S. oil companies to boycott Iranian crude, which decimated its exports. Mossadegh suggested he might find markets for the oil in the communist Soviet Union. President Dwight D. Eisenhower did not take the hint lightly and helped overthrow Mossadegh. The Central Intelligence Agency's Kermit Roosevelt, the cousin of Franklin Roosevelt, hid under a blanket on the floor of a car to sneak into the palace of Shah Mohammad Reza Pahlavi. Roosevelt convinced the shah, who once had greater

Kermit Roosevelt

power over Iran , and convinced him that America would back him if he seized control. In August 1953, the CIA helped support public demonstrations for the shah that flooded the streets, and Mossadegh surrendered.

When the shah returned to power, Britain lost its dominant share in Anglo-Iranian Oil Company. BP got 40 percent and the U.S. companies got the rest. A new Iranian-owned oil company became the executive owner of the country's petroleum resources.

Another major conflict had been brewing in the Middle East. Beginning in the 1880s, many Jews fled from persecution in Eastern Europe to Israel, which was sacred to them. With the spread of Nazism in Germany beginning in the 1930s and its persecution of Jews, a new wave of Jewish immigration came to Palestine from Eastern Europe. Palestine, which was controlled by Britain, was sacred to Arabs. Feeling threatened by the fresh immigration, Arabs bombed Jewish settlements. The Jews fought back.

Following the defeat of Germany in World War II, President Harry S. Truman sent an immigration official to Europe to get a report about the plight of the Jews there in the aftermath of the Nazi concentration camps. Their poor living conditions made him urge the British to permit 100,000 Jews to immigrate to Palestine.

Frustrated, the British turned the future of Palestine over to the newly formed United Nations. More than two-thirds of the global body voted for partition and in May 1948, it announced the state of Israel. Eleven minutes later Truman, who was eager for Jewish support in his own country, issued a statement recognizing the new country.

# Chapter Four
# Boom Times to Growth Limits

S uddenly oil started to flood global markets from the Middle East and beyond. In the 1950s Saudi Arabia and Iran boosted production and so did the United States and the Soviet Union. The abundance started pushing down petroleum prices and consumers rejoiced. Across the United States oil demand boomed as Americans fell in love with big cars. At the end of the war 10 million veterans had returned from the war to the delight of car companies. And cars were cheap: just one-hundred dollars and an agreement to make three years of payments put a slick powerful gas guzzler in the driveway.

The road was fertile ground for new businesses. The first Holiday Inn opened in 1952, and in 1955 a milkshake machine salesman named Ray Kroc opened the first modern McDonald's restaurant in Illinois. Eight years later five hundred McDonald's dotted the nation's busiest roads. Suburbanization, which had begun in the 1920s, but faltered during the Great Depression and the war, resumed at a greater pace as cars made it easy for workers to commute.

Eisenhower pushed through the Interstate Highway Act in 1956. Spanning twenty years of projects and eventually costing more than $100 billion, it was the largest U.S. public works program to date. The act called for a system of highways so the military could mobilize in the event of an attack. Shopping centers, motels, and gas stations became part of everyday life.

By 1960, U.S. owners had registered about 74 million cars, nearly double the number ten years earlier. Lifestyles revolved around the car. Drive-in movie theaters drew parking lots full of people. In addition, oil was being used for new things beyond transportation fuel: making plastics, as a replacement for coal in power plants, and for heating homes. For a while it seemed oil's promise could only get better.

The price collapse wasn't good for everyone, though. U.S. oil companies operating in the Middle East were feeling squeezed, especially because by the end of the 1950s the Soviet Union had become the world's second largest oil producer. They couldn't raise prices because other companies would undersell them. So oil companies led by Exxon cut the prices at which they would buy crude from their Middle Eastern host producers by up to 14 cents a barrel, or about 7 percent. They had hoped to force the producers to share the price of competing with the Soviet Union.

It was a mistake. In 1960, representatives from the countries that exported 80 percent of the world's oil, Saudi Arabia, Kuwait, Iran, Iraq, and Venezuela met in Baghdad. Over six days they formed a new group—the Organization of the Petroleum Exporting Countries (OPEC)—committed to solidarity in defending the price of oil against companies and consumers like the United States.

It took the Six-Day War of 1967 to spur Arab oil producers to action. Egypt had led a mobilization of Arab military might and

blockades that threatened Israel's ability to import oil. On June 5, Israel attacked, capturing new territories, including all of Jerusalem and the West Bank. In response, the Arab oil producers unleashed their "oil weapon" by halting shipments to nations friendly to Israel including the United States, Britain, and West Germany.

But the results of the first major oil embargo were less than spectacular. U.S. President Lyndon Johnson organized energy companies to ensure steady supplies. Huge Japanese-built "supertankers" that had been built a decade before provided

unexpected relief by transporting oil from non-Arab producers to consumer countries. Oil production surged in Venezuela
and in the United States, which had long limited production to
save oil in the event of an emergency. Fearing a loss of business from the development of extra oil, the Arab exporters
lifted the embargo.

Just a few years later it became apparent that the United
States couldn't produce its way out of trouble forever. In 1970
U.S. oil production peaked at 9.6 million bpd as big fields

began to run dry and has since fallen to about 5 million bpd. The government lifted the output limits, but even that wasn't enough. "Texas oil fields have been like a reliable old warrior that could rise to the task when needed," said the chairman of the Texas Railroad Commission, which regulated oil production in the state. "That old warrior can't rise anymore."

OPEC could almost sense the demise of oil production in the world's biggest energy consumer before it happened. At a 1968 meeting, producers pledged within five years that they—not the oil companies and consumer countries — would set petroleum prices. They knew they held the cards — by 1972, one third of U.S. oil came from the Middle East.

Producers in the Middle East insisted on taking shares of the national oil companies themselves, not just some of their profits. They viewed the concession system as a continuation of the exploitation of their own resources that had occurred since colonial times. In Iraq, the military regime shocked oil companies by nationalizing the Iraq Petroleum Company without compensation. Saudi Arabia was hungry for a share of Aramco that was owned by U.S. oil companies, but the king also saw reason for not pushing too hard. The Oil Minister Sheikh Yamani argued against full nationalization, knowing the companies had developed markets and global distribution systems over many decades. The kingdom needed their expertise. And he did not want to needlessly anger the United States which might turn quickly to new supplies. A solid friendship with the United States could help make the kingdom more secure through military protection and the sale of weapons.

Saudi Arabia and the U.S. companies agreed to a 25 percent participation rate of the kingdom in Aramco that would rise to 51 percent by 1983. Companies in the Middle East feared the agreement would lead to other governments taking bigger chunks. Sure enough, Libya's Muammar al-Qaddafi took over 50 percent of the Italian state oil company operating in his region. Then he took 51 percent of the Libyan investments of U.S. oil company Occidental, boasting he had given the United States a "big hard blow" on "its cold insolent face."

Tensions mounted as world demand grew and the price of oil doubled between 1970 and 1973. The Arab states produced more of the world's oil and looked to transform their growing petroleum moneys into political power. They talked about using the "oil weapon" again to hold back exports, raise prices, and shift more capital into the Middle East.

As Arab-Israeli violence festered, Saudi Arabia's King Faisal was determined to win back Jerusalem, the third-holiest site for Muslims which had been lost to Israel in the 1967 war. In August of 1973, Syrian and Egyptian leaders decided they would launch the next Arab-Israeli war in October, and Faisal promised to use the oil weapon if war broke out.

The king may have feared uprisings in Saudi Arabia. Radicals seeking restoration of their homelands in Palestine had tried to bomb oil installations in the kingdom and might eventually challenge the monarchy itself. To quell them, Faisal pressured the United States to push Israel to withdraw from the territories. His oil minister met with U.S. officials and warned of a change in oil policy if it did not take such steps.

Saudi Arabia had newfound clout. It had recently surpassed Texas as the world's largest petroleum producer. That meant it was the only country with enough reserves to supply petroleum to global consumers in the event of emergencies that slowed output from other producers.

Meanwhile President Richard Nixon's plate was heaped with other issues. The United States was locked in the Cold War with the Soviet Union. At home Nixon was under fire for helping to cover up break-ins by his loyalists at the Democrat's national headquarters and other corrupt acts known as the Watergate scandal.

U.S. dependence on imported oil had jumped. But few in Washington foresaw the risk. When Exxon officials told the White House in May 1973 that King Faisal might soon use the oil weapon, they were told, "His Majesty is calling wolf where no wolf exists except in his imagination." As agreed, Egypt and Syria attacked Israel in October. Days later Saudi Arabia's Yamani announced OPEC was raising the price of Persian Gulf oil by 70 percent to $5.10 a barrel.

In response to the attacks, Nixon proposed $2.2 billion in military aid to Israel. He aimed to balance power in the Middle East so that both Israel and Egypt would have to come to the negotiating table. But the aid infuriated OPEC's Arab members. On top of cut backs that hit the entire global market, they announced a total ban on exported oil to the United States (and the Netherlands) until Israel gave up territories.

In December, OPEC raised oil to $11.65 a barrel, or four times its price before the war. The shah of Iran was eager for new income to help solidify his rule and pushed for the high prices. But even he listened to advisers who said a price above

$11.65 would push consumers to develop alternative sources of energy like liquid fuels from coal and shale, of which the United States had big supplies.

The price spike meant the Arab exporters could sell less but earn more. It also increased demand for oil by encouraging U.S. refiners and other customers to buy more petroleum to sock away in tanks on the bet it would only become more valuable over time.

Consumers in the United States felt the first global oil crisis quickly. The country had just 6 percent of the world's population in 1973 but consumed a third of global oil supplies. The free, open road got all gummed up. Motorists fearful of running out of gas waited in lines, occasionally four miles long, at stations night after night to top off their tanks. "Sorry, No Gas" signs at stations sprouted up.

Many stations blocked access to the pumps, offering only a narrow passage for regular customers. One evening at a Connecticut station "the pumps were barricaded tonight by a wrecker, a blue Buick, a panel truck, a purple Jeep, a red Volkswagen, a blue and white Scout, two garbage cans, two oil drums and a saw horse." Some stations in New York City gave preferential treatment for people such as diplomats, doctors, and police, which made it even harder for regular people to fill up. As tempers rose, New York City stationed police at the busiest stations. New York and New Jersey passed laws in which cars that had license plates that ended with odd numbers could only fill up on odd- numbered days of the month and vice versa.

During the winter of 1973, many Americans were also fearful they wouldn't be able afford oil keep their homes warm. Two U.S. congressmen who visited Yamani in Riyadh said the oil minister threatened to use heating oil as a weapon too. "This winter, when there is a shortage of fuel in the United States and your people begin to suffer—the change will begin. Americans are not used to being uncomfortable," he was quoted as saying.

With the impact shortages could have on daily life, people began wondering how long the world's oil supply would last. Millions bought a 1972 book called *The Limits to Growth*. Coming just two years after U.S. oil production peaked, it was based on computer models that warned society would face a disastrous collapse in one hundred years from pollution and the depletion of resources like metals and oil. The book met with criticism from some economists who said the models did not account for technology that could develop new sources of energy. And some felt waste, not a growing population, was the problem. But combined with the high oil prices and gas lines, the book spurred the public to think about resources as finite. It was a new way of thinking in the United States where the splendors of the vast lands had seemed limitless.

Pollution had already helped focus the environmental movement, after California suffered several ill effects from oil dependence. In 1969, a drilling platform suffered a blow-out in the Santa Barbara channel, causing millions of gallons of oil to bubble up from the sea bottom. The slick coated the shore, which was littered with dead fish and birds. It galvanized the beach communities to help clean the mess and fight offshore drilling.

In the 1960s, tailpipe emissions from Los Angeles freeways caused record levels of smog resulting in poor visibility and health problems. The state enacted the toughest clean air standards in the country and shifted from burning coal and oil in power plants to cleaner natural gas.

Nixon became the first U.S. president to urge energy independence, and he turned the 1973 White House Christmas tree into a symbol of his plan. The tree shone with a single light that season. "This year we will drive a little slower," he said at the lighting ceremony. "This year the thermostats will be a little lower." Later he declared America would provide its own energy by 1980. Utilities burned coal instead of oil. He pledged $10 billion for energy research and development. The government lowered speed limits to increase car mileage and

licensed nuclear power plants. Meanwhile commuters took trains and buses and formed car pools.

Conservation helped the country use less oil, but by the time the embargo was lifted in March the economic damage was already set in motion. Two decades of prosperity that had given way to months of panic were followed by years of recession. U.S. gasoline and heating oil prices had risen 33 percent in some places. Unemployment hit 8.5 percent by 1975, the highest level since World War II. By the end of the decade, inflation and unemployment rates both soared into the double digits.

The recession threatened the might of the global powerhouse. As the oil historian Daniel Yergin put it "the United States, the world's foremost superpower and underwriter of the international order, had now been thrown on the defensive, humiliated, by a handful of small nations."

To defend themselves from future oil price shocks, many Western consumer countries, including the United States, banded together to form the Paris-based International Energy Agency in 1974. It was charged with coordinating supply measures in any future energy crises and setting targets for countries to build emergency oil reserves.

In 1975, the U.S. Congress authorized the Strategic Petroleum Reserve, directing it to store about three month's worth of imports, with an initial goal of five hundred million barrels. Congress considered a variety of ideas about where to store the oil, including giant rubber bags, until deciding upon underground salt caverns in Louisiana. The caverns held more than seven hundred million barrels in early 2009.

For the OPEC countries, the mid-1970s brought vast new wealth as they completed the nationalization of their resources. Petroleum earnings for the group's exporters rose from $23 billion in 1972 to $140 billion by 1977 with much of it spent on weaponry to maintain their newfound power. They also purchased hotels, telephone systems, and trucks and cars.

The creeping nationalization of oil resources among OPEC members became a sprint. In 1974, the shah nationalized the National Iranian Oil Company. Soon after that Kuwait and Venezuela nationalized their oil industries. All that was left was Aramco. Saudi Arabia had taken 60 percent of the company and now wanted all of it. In 1976, after a year of negotiations with Sheik Yamani, Chevron, Exxon, Mobil, and Texaco agreed to turn over Aramco to the kingdom in exchange for the right to market 80 percent of its output. The multinational oil companies that had built the Persian Gulf industry and once owned the oil in the ground were now becoming mere contractors to the oil-producing nations. Between 1974 and 1978, Persian Gulf oil rose from about $12 a barrel to $15.

Higher oil prices and the threat of tightening OPEC control spurred consumer countries to embark on greater efforts to control their energy imports and demand. Congress approved opening the Trans Alaskan Pipeline. The eight hundred-mile duct had been in the works since the largest oilfield in North America was discovered on Alaska's North Slope in 1968. But Alaskan native groups and

The Trans Alaskan Pipeline

environmentalists had helped block the building of the line for five years. With Congress's approval the building of the line resumed, and the taps opened in 1977. Tankers took crude from the line's end at the Port of Valdez to the West Coast and Japan.

Congress in 1975 enacted CAFE standards, short for Corporate Average Fuel Economy, that required car makers to more than double fuel efficiency from thirteen miles per gallon in ten years.

Jimmy Carter became president in 1977 and made energy conservation one of his top issues. Just three months into his administration he gave a fireside chat introducing his energy policy while wearing a cardigan sweater. In the

President Jimmy Carter

speech, he called decisions about energy the "moral equivalent of war." Carter called for a reduction in gasoline consumption of 10 percent and an increase in coal production. He ordered the swelling of the national Strategic Petroleum Reserve to 1 billion barrels.

He emphasized conservation through efficient cars, increased use of public transportation, and insulation of homes to prevent heat from escaping. He also called for the use of solar energy in 2.5 million homes. Later in 1979, in the first press conference on the roof of the White House, he unveiled a $28,000 solar cell system that heated some of the executive mansion's water. Conservation laws enacted by Presidents Gerald Ford and Carter cut per capita oil consumption by Americans 23 percent between 1978 and 1983.

By 1978, 1 million bpd were coming down the Alaskan pipe and a few years later 2 million, a quarter of U.S. production at the time. The high prices also led to a new rush to find global oil supplies. Having been marginalized by OPEC countries, the multinational companies now set their sites on the West. Mexico, whose population was surging and economy was in a shambles, began to sell exports again.

Oil producers developed an even bigger bonanza beneath the rough frigid waters of the North Sea between Britain and Norway. BP, Exxon, and Shell all invested in rigs that could drill for oil thousands of feet below the surface. Offshore drilling in such conditions was dangerous and claimed many lives. But the pressure on companies to find new supplies led to technological advances and ensured deep sea drilling as an important new source of oil. In 1975, the first oil from the North Sea flowed from a tanker to a British refinery.

Higher oil prices also led to conflict. In Iran, money from oil sales that flooded in during the mid-1970s hindered the shah's modernization campaign. People from rural towns poured into the cities looking for jobs. City streets could

The Ayatollah Khomeini

not handle the swarms of new cars and the train system was swamped. Food production fell and inflation was rampant.

Islamic fundamentalism grew. Many activists never forgot a lavish bash the shah had thrown in 1971 for world leaders celebrating the 2,500th anniversary of the founding of the Persian Empire that had gone on despite a drought that had led to starvation for many. The Ayatollah Khomeini, a lecturer on Islamic philosophy, had railed since the 1960s against the shah's modernization plan, protests that eventually exiled him to Iraq.

From there he became the harshest critic of the shah, calling him a puppet of the United States. In January 1978, riots broke out in Iran's Qom, the spiritual home of Khomeini, in which several students died. Thereafter, sympathizers carried out protests every forty days in accordance with mourning traditions.

In August fundamentalists set a half dozen movie theaters around the country on fire for showing "sinful" films full of "western propaganda." The protests grew bigger and moved to Tehran. In December, millions of protestors flooded the capital city and called for the return of Khomeini. Thousands died in clashes with security forces.

Finally the sick and weakened shah fled Iran in January. In February, Khomeini flew back to Tehran and created the Islamic Republic of Iran. His rise to power was watched with apprehension in the United States, but also in Saudi Arabia. After all, Khomeini's republic represented Shi'a Muslim instead of Sunni interests, directly threatening Saudi Arabia's "position as the international mouthpiece for the Prophet Muhammad." It also made clear that a religious leader could replace a long established monarchy.

The revolution in the second-largest exporter of oil after Saudi Arabia brought about the world's second oil crisis in which prices shot from about thirteen dollars a barrel to thirty-six dollars a barrel. Uncertainty about the security of oil supplies led again to panic. For consumers it seemed that 1979 was a continuation of the 1973 crisis and the days of cheap oil were gone forever.

Suddenly in November 1979, a group of three hundred militant students in Tehran took the U.S. embassy, kidnapping about fifty hostages. They demanded that the shah, who was in a New York hospital suffering from cancer, be sent back to Iran to go on trial. A spokesman for Khomeini said the occupation of the embassy had his personal support.

The kidnappers held the hostages for 444 days. Each night on the news, U.S. television viewers watched militants shouting slogans such as "Death to America."

At the beginning of the hostage crisis, Carter used the only tools at his disposal—economic penalties. He banned imports of Iranian oil to the United States and froze Iranian assets. Iran responded by halting exports to any U.S.-based multinational oil company.

The halt only accounted for about 5 percent of the world's 50 million bpd global oil market, but it led to chaos. Long-term contracts between producers and consumers, which had led to price stability, were cancelled. Once again, long lines full of gas guzzling cars snaked out from U.S. filling stations.

By April 1980, Carter had lost patience. He ordered an assault on the hostage takers by eight helicopters aided by air-planes. One of the helicopters got lost, one had mechanical failures, and one crashed in the Iranian desert, killing several U.S. soldiers. Carter called off the attack and the militants quickly dispersed the hostages throughout the country.

During the crisis OPEC production actually rose in 1979, as Saudi Arabia and others boosted output. The extra oil went to feed rising demand, but also some energy companies stored the oil in hopes the price would go still higher and they could make a profit. By 1980, some oil companies even stored their extra crude in supertankers, regardless of the huge expense.

In September of that year, OPEC leaders gathered near the group's headquarters in Vienna to plan a celebration in Baghdad of the twentieth anniversary of the group's found-ing. But in Baghdad, Iraq's president Saddam Hussein had something else planned.

The oil ministers' meeting erupted into chaos as news broke that Iraqi jets had bombed Iran's navy. Hussein said the attacks were meant to stop Khomeini's revolution from spreading across the Middle East. But the conflict had many causes including power struggles that went back 5,000 years. There were also border disputes, worsened by the carving up of the Middle East by colonial powers after the defeat of the Ottoman Empire in World War I.

There was bad blood between the Khomeini and Hussein, both of whom had come to power in 1979. They came from different sides of the Muslim faith, Khomeini was a Shi'a, while Hussein was a Sunni, both of which argued they were the successor line to the Prophet Muhammad. And Hussein was hungry for power throughout the Middle East. One of the goals of his Ba'th party was to create one Arab nation that opposed imperialism and the West.

On the second day of the war, Iraqi jets bombed Iranian refineries—one of which was the world's largest. Then Iraq bombed all of Iran's oil ports. Iran struck back stopping Iraqi oil exports altogether, which gave world oil prices yet another pop.

OPEC broke into two factions. One, including Saudi Arabia, argued that too-high prices would hurt demand, while the other faction, including Iran, shot back that the industrialized countries could afford higher prices. "Two of our members are dropping bombs on each other," a diplomat from one of the OPEC countries said at the meeting "and many of the rest of us cannot agree on even the basics of our trade."

Despite the war, the oil market soon calmed as other producers opened their taps. Saudi Arabia increased production. So did Russia, Mexico, Norway, and Britain. Output from Alaska hit about 1.6 million bpd in 1981 and rose for the next seven years. "The oil weapon, employed by OPEC to such devastating effect in 1973-74 and again in 1979 . . . has lately turned into a boomerang," the *New York Times* said in March 1982. Indeed, that year non-OPEC oil production overtook OPEC output for the first time, forcing the cartel to come up with a new strategy to keep their grip on world oil prices. So the group decided to limit oil production to 18 million bpd. All the producers, except Saudi Arabia, which was to act as the market balancer, were saddled with limits. Only three years earlier the group had pumped 31 million bpd.

Yet the output caps weren't ambitious enough. High quality oil that refiners desired because it was easy to process into motor fuels continued to gush from the North Sea. Some OPEC members cut their prices to compete. But the largest producer, Saudi Arabia, refused to budge. Consumers turned to other sources of oil and the kingdom's output fell to its lowest level since 1970. In 1983, OPEC also cut oil prices by 15 percent, the first time it had done so as a group.

Later that year there was more bad news for OPEC and it didn't come from the oil fields of Mexico or Russia or the North Sea, but from a commodities market in downtown New York City that got its start in dairy products. Merchants had founded The Butter and Cheese Exchange of New York in 1872 to make trading of those products easier. In 1920, egg futures were added. The baker who invested in egg futures could now be sure of what his expenses would be months into the future instead of being vulnerable to daily price swings. After World War II, potatoes became the top commodity on the bourse, which was now known as the New York Mercantile Exchange (NYMEX). In 1977, however, the crop failed, leaving it with mounds of rotten potatoes. So NYMEX leaders decided to launch a futures contract for trading heating oil to help small distributors of the fuel around New York deal with the powerful oil companies.

Then it developed its biggest energy futures contract of all, crude oil.

The official prices of crude and fuels were soon hashed out by mobs of shouting and wildly gesticulating traders in the "pits" of the windowless cavern of the NYMEX. Today traders are addicted to the headlines about everything from OPEC oil output, U.S. energy supplies, war, weather, and politics that flash on the electronic boards covering the exchange's walls. A government report of a surprise jump in U.S. crude supplies, for instance, can send prices down. A production cut by a big OPEC producer can send it up minutes later.

NYMEX trade reduced secretive oil deals between Middle Eastern producers and global consumers in which buyers never really knew if they were getting a good price. OPEC and other producers still had power over the price of oil, but now information was shared widely and deals were less murky.

With the emergence of futures markets and the extra non-OPEC oil, energy became a back-burner issue in global politics. OPEC countries squabbled about their output quotas at the group's meetings and cheated on the limits in private, pumping more oil than they were allowed. The cheating led to more oil in the markets which pushed prices down. To make matters worse, alternative sources of energy including coal, nuclear power, and natural gas took market share away from oil that was burned at power plants to generate electricity.

The oil price began to fall. Iran and Iraq boosted output even though they were still at war. By the mid-1980s Saudi Arabia, which had operated as a swing producer, keeping prices high by reducing its own output, was growing tired of the sacrifice. In 1985 even North Sea production at times was more than that from Saudi Arabia, the oil giant of the Middle East. In fact non-OPEC oil had risen to 69 percent of world output by 1985, compared to 50 percent in 1978. With the drop in exports from the Middle East, some of the world's largest supertankers that had carried Persian Gulf oil to the United States since the 1970s were cut up for scrap.

In December 1985, Saudi Arabia abandoned its swing producer strategy. Saudi Arabia now sought to make money by grabbing a bigger share of the market. It did that by opening the taps and flooding the market with oil that was less expensive to drill than everyone else's. It boosted output from a twenty-year low of 2.2 million bpd to between 4.5 million and 5 million bpd. With all the new output coming from the North Sea, Alaska, and Mexico, the kingdom's move led to the next oil shock. Global oil prices dropped 70 percent in a few months from nearly thirty-two dollars a barrel in late 1985 to ten dollars.

Americans wondered how low oil prices would go, which led to changes from the refinery to the gas station. Refiners no longer believed oil would rise so they stopped storing it, which cut demand even further. Gasoline station antics made headlines again. Instead of drivers battling to get to the head of the line, gas station owners fought each other for who could sell fuel at the lowest price. On highways in New Jersey, for instance, some station owners called the police to stop their competitors from setting up large sandwich board signs that showed off their gasoline prices.

While consumers enjoyed the low gasoline prices, oil producers, except Saudi Arabia, were hurting. The low oil prices caused slowdowns in the North Sea and Alaska, where oil was expensive to pump. In Russia, then the world's largest oil producer, the drop in prices slashed income and slowed oil production.

Most regions in the United States were enjoying the low oil prices, especially the East and West coasts. Producers in Texas, however, were suffering. Energy companies slashed jobs and banks teetered. Luckily for them, the oil patch had a very powerful friend.

George H.W. Bush, the father of George W. Bush, had moved to Texas after graduating from Yale. Using his own father's connections got a job sweeping warehouses and working on pumps for an oil company. He eventually formed an oil company which made him a millionaire. He was elected a U.S. congressman and later moved to higher positions including director of the Central Intelligence Agency. In 1980, Ronald Reagan picked Bush to be his vice president.

When oil collapsed to less than ten dollars a barrel in 1986, Bush traveled to the Middle East. He believed cheap oil imports were threatening U.S. security because they were shutting down the country's own ability to pump oil. The low prices increased the country's demand for fuel, but crippled production in the Southwest. During the trip Bush broke with Reagan's policy of free markets—that the government should not interfere with prices. At a dinner he told the Saudi oil minister Yamani that if prices stayed low it might be difficult to stop the U.S. Congress from pushing for a fee on every barrel of oil coming into the country that would help U.S. producers compete.

Extremely low oil prices also gave Saudi Arabia pause. If they fell much further the loss of revenues to the kingdom could be severe. Saudi Arabia feared that if pressure was growing within the United States for an import tariff other countries that had made progress on alternatives to oil, such as Japan had with nuclear power, would call for tariffs too.

At its next meeting, OPEC members decided there was a right price for oil. Ten dollars a barrel was too low and thirty dollars would drive consumers to conserve. The ministers agreed eighteen dollars a barrel was the reasonable price. Big consumers were relatively happy with the target. OPEC agreed to a new quota system and Saudi Arabia stopped flooding the market. Even non-OPEC producers such as the Soviet Union, China, Mexico, and others agreed to hold back production.

The agreement worked. Prices began rising in 1987 and held steady through 1989. In the U.S. Southwest, the relief was palpable. "People are starting to say, 'Thank God, I'm going to have a future,' '' said an oilman in Midland, Texas. Meanwhile, Iran-Iraq fighting had developed into a tanker war with both sides hitting belligerent ships as well as neutral ones. Iran hit tankers from Kuwait, an ally of Iraq's. That prompted Kuwait to ask the United States for naval protection of its ships. Washington readily agreed as it was afraid if it didn't do the job the other superpower, communist Soviet Union, would.

By the summer of 1988, both Iran and Iraq were spent from war. Iran had few allies and little chance of winning. It proposed a cease-fire and after much negotiation the two sides agreed to a truce in August after an estimated 500,000 to 1.5 million had died. Yet little was resolved. Iraq emerged as the victor and as the strongest military force in the region behind Israel, but an arms race and power struggle continued.

Relations between oil producers and consumers, meanwhile, could almost be described as friendly. U.S. motorists were paying the least amount for fuel, adjusted for inflation, than they had for decades. OPEC members such as Kuwait and the United Arab Emirates produced well over their quotas which helped push oil prices several dollars below the group's eighteen dollars a barrel target.

As a result, conservation moved to the back burner. Overall gas mileage for U.S. sedans hadn't improved significantly since 1983. At 27.5 miles per gallon, fuel economy was on the way to holding steady for the next sixteen years. And in 1986, the Reagan administration removed Carter's solar panels from the White House during "roof repairs."

# The Dwight D. Eisenhower System of Interstate and Defense Highways

In the summer of 1919, a convoy of eighty-one Army motorcycles, trucks, and cars set out on a transcontinental trip. It was the first trip of its kind for the Army, which wanted to test its fleet and determine how easy or difficult it would be to cross the North American continent. The starting point of the journey was a place south of the White House, known as "Zero Milestone." The end point was San Francisco, 3,000 miles away.

The vehicles were accompanied by a fifteen-piece band (provided by Goodyear Tire and Rubber), twenty-four Army officers, and 258 enlisted men, including a young lieutenant colonel named Dwight D. Eisenhower, who later wrote that he went along "partly for a lark and partly to learn. We were not sure it could be accomplished at all. Nothing of the sort had ever been attempted."

Sixty-two days later the caravan finally arrived in San Francisco, after enduring more than 230 road accidents—everything from overturned vehicles to vehicles stuck in quicksand and mud. The expedition made a lasting impression on Eisenhower, who described

the trip as a journey "through darkest America with truck and tank." Conditions on the road, he said, ranged "from average to non-existent."

Eisenhower never forgot that experience, but it was his time in Europe, as Supreme Allied Commander during World War II, that set in motion "thinking about good, two-lane highways." Eisenhower was especially impressed by Adolf Hitler's autobahn, so when he became president of the United States, "I decided ... to put an emphasis upon this kind of road building."

Planning for a highway system had begun in the 1930s and in 1944 President Franklin D. Roosevelt had pushed for a national system. But it was not until Eisenhower took office that the plan began to take shape. On June 29, 1956, Eisenhower signed the $25-billion Federal-Aid Highway Act, authorizing the creation of a 41,000-mile highway system to connect the whole country, by 1972.

The interstate highway system (later formally named the Dwight D. Eisenhower System of Interstate and Defense Highways) is the largest public works program in American history. It took more than forty years to build, at a cost

of more than $130 billion. By 1960, four years after Eisenhower signed the act, more than 10,000 miles were open to traffic. By 1980, 40,000 miles of interstate highway were open, and today that figure stands at 46,876 miles. And, because of the highway system, the drive time between the nation's capital and San Francisco is less than forty-eight hours, thanks to Interstate 80, which takes drivers through the states of Pennsylvania, Ohio, Indiana, Illinois, Iowa, Nebraska, Wyoming, Utah, and Nevada.

Almost all major urban areas in the U.S. are connected to one another by the interstate highway network. And though the interstate system only represents about 1 percent of the nation's roadway network, it carries 23 percent of all roadway traffic. By reducing travel time between cities, the interstate system has transformed America. ■

# Beyond Oil: Coal to Liquids

With no oil of its own and very few friends around the world, South Africa's racist government narrowly escaped disaster after 1979, when Iran stopped shipping it oil after a revolution splintered its energy business. Other countries refused to sell oil to South Africa in an attempt to strangle apartheid, in which the country forced blacks off their land and revoked their citizenship.

Perhaps sensing that one day its racism would make it an unpopular business partner, South Africa's National Party instituted a state energy company called Sasol back in 1950. Sasol improved methods to make diesel from coal, using techniques invented in the 1920s by the Germans Franz Fischer and Hans Tropsch. The process uses heat and pressure to break coal down into a gas and then into liquid fuel. The Nazis exploited the process during World War II to fuel its military. South Africa perfected it. Apartheid died in 1994, but South Africa's cars, trucks, and planes still get fuel from coal.

Now, amid worries about the future of oil, coal-to-liquids (CTL) is getting another look. China, the United States, and Australia all plan to build CTL plants. But CTL has environmental flaws. It produces about double the emissions of the greenhouse gas carbon dioxide as petroleum fuels. And the process uses lots of water, which can be problematic in deserts where some of the plants are being proposed. Unless engineers develop ways to recycle the water and store the emissions permanently underground, CTL faces an uncertain future.

Even so, companies and politicians are urging plants to be built, eager to enhance national security by making domes-

Sasol, founded in 1950, is the world's largest producer of synthetic fuels. Pictured here is a Sasol Slurry Phase reactor, where waxes and distillate fuels are produced.

tic fuel. In China, the world's largest coal consumer, the state-owned Shenhua Group plans to build a plant in Inner Mongolia. If it succeeds, the region will embark on a plan to convert half of its coal output into fuels and chemicals. As China gets more cars the pressure to succeed builds. "We cannot fail," said Zhang Jiming, a deputy general manager at Shenhua.

CTL is also enticing to entrepreneurs in United States, which boasts the world's largest coal supplies and where there is pressure to cut dependence on foreign oil. About a dozen plants are planned throughout the country. DRKW Advanced Fuels plans to start construction on a plant in Wyoming in partnership with Arch Coal Inc. And the U.S. Air Force is experimenting with CTL. The fuel has a shelf life of about 15 years, which means it could be socked away in secret locations for future military operations.

In Montana, the Native American Crow tribe recently signed an agreement with the Australian-American Energy Co. to develop a $7 billion CTL plant called Many Stars. They hope to begin making 50,000 barrels of oil sometime in the next decade. Governor Brian Schweitzer backs the project. West Virginia and Kentucky are also looking into making liquid fuels from coal.

Some projects to help store the carbon dioxide stripped from natural gas have been underway for years. Norway's StatoilHydro has been pumping about 1 million tons a year of carbon dioxide into a reservoir under the North Sea since 1996. Perhaps some of the emissions from CTL could be pumped into aging U.S. oil fields. But there's also a big risk of oversupply. If the United States regulates greenhouse gases, carbon storage may be part of the effort to fight global warming. But the country's six hundred conventional coal-burning plants emit far more carbon dioxide than has been stored in the North Sea.

Engineers say the gas could be stored in deep underground saline formations that are spread throughout the United States. The formations are also common in China, but less so in India, another big coal consumer. But nobody knows how billions of tons of carbon dioxide would react underground, whether it would hurt underground water supplies or find ways to escape to the atmosphere.

Even if the carbon dioxide could be safely stored, coal mining can be a dirty and dangerous business. In the eastern United States, coal companies blow off the tops of mountains with dynamite. Giant machines push excess rock and dirt the industry calls "overburden" down into the streams below.

Oil's future price may ultimately dictate how fast CTL develops. As the South Africa case shows, some business models benefit from desperation. ■

# Chapter Five
# What's Left?

A close look at global oil supplies showed some troubling developments. While U.S. oil production had risen through the mid-1980s with the addition of the Alaskan pipeline, by 1988 Alaskan oil had peaked. That same year, total U.S. production had fallen below 3 billion barrels per year for the first time in eleven years and it has declined almost every year since, to current levels of less than 2 billion barrels per year. As production fell in the late 1980s dependence grew on imports, much of which came from the Middle East.

Iraq's president Saddam Hussein believed that quota cheating by other OPEC members was keeping the price of oil too low and robbing his country of riches. In July 1990, he said the oil export policies of fellow Arab producers Kuwait and the United Arab Emirates were directed by Americans seeking low energy prices and he threatened them with force. "Iraqis will not forget the saying that cutting necks is better than cutting means of living," he said. "O God almighty, be witness that we have warned them."

In early August, Hussein's troops invaded Kuwait, taking Kuwait City and the country's top oil fields in twelve hours. The grab made Iraq the world's top oil producer, with a quarter of the world's oil reserves. Hussein wanted Iraq to be the dominant force in the Middle East both militarily and economically, a force on par with the biggest powers in the West.

Saddam Hussein with Venezuelan president Hugo Chavez, who angered the U.S. when he became the first head of state to visit Iraq after the 1991 war. *(Courtesy of AP Images/INA)*

The U.S. response to the attacks was swift. President George H. W. Bush helped secure a U.N. resolution condemning the invasion four days after it occurred. After getting permission from Saudi Arabia's king Fahd, Bush moved warplanes and ground troops to the kingdom. Iraqi troops had lined part of the kingdom's border too, so Bush didn't have to do much convincing.

Iraq ignored another U.N. resolution calling for withdrawal from Kuwait by January 15. Days later, Bush announced that the United States and allied forces had bombed targets in Iraq and Kuwait.

What followed was like a scene from hell. Iraqi troops dumped crude into the Persian Gulf and began setting Kuwaiti refineries and oil fields alight. Some of the smoky infernos took more than a year to douse. Allied ground forces invaded Iraq and Kuwait in February. Hussein quickly ordered troops to withdraw. Allied forces bombed the retreating troops, killing Iraqi soldiers and their Kuwaiti hostages. Charred bodies and twisted vehicles littered the stretch of road that became known as the "highway of death." U.S. and Saudi troops entered Kuwait City on February 27. Bush declared liberation and then weeks later a cease-fire.

On January 16, the day that Bush had announced the bombings, he let it be known that the United States would begin its first emergency use of its oil reserve to help calm prices. The next day oil prices dropped more than ten dollars to twenty-one dollars a barrel, at the time the largest price drop ever recorded.

After the war, Iraq produced far less oil. But rising output in other countries brought the problem of the global surplus to the surface again, along with more bickering between OPEC members about how and when to cut back. The early

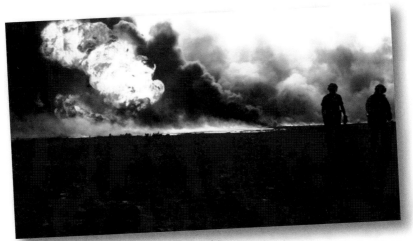

Two soldiers stand in the distance as an oil field burns during Operation Desert Storm, in Kuwait.
(Courtesy Jonas Jordan/U.S. Army Corps of Engineers)

This January 1991 photo shows a reflection of fire in oil burning at Burgan Oil Field in Kuwait during the Gulf War. According to recent reports, Burgan, the second-largest oil field in the world, is starting to run out of oil. *(Courtesy National Oceanic and Atmospheric Administration)* to mid-1990s were dominated by comparatively low and stable oil prices as supply outweighed demand.

While consumers enjoyed relatively low oil prices, a growing movement questioned the world's dependence on fossil fuels. One sultry June day in 1988, NASA scientist James Hansen testified to a Senate committee that he had "99 percent confidence" that the global temperature was rising and human-made greenhouse gases from burning of fossil fuels and other activities were almost surely responsible. Scientists already knew that carbon dioxide from tail pipes and smokestacks trapped the sun's heat in the atmosphere causing the greenhouse effect. But Hansen's testimony, given on a day in which temperatures soared past one hundred degrees in forty-five U.S. cities, drilled the point home. The summer's heat wave caused an estimated 5,000 to 10,000 deaths across the United States and drought damaged tens of billions of dollars worth of crops and related industries.

The planet had gone through periods of climate change many times before that had taken tens of thousands of years. Now, Hansen reasoned, people had the potential to warm the climate over tens of years. That could add wallop to hurricanes, cause deadly floods in low-lying areas as icebergs melt, and droughts and heat waves in higher areas.

As the public gradually became concerned, many energy companies did too. Companies such as Exxon and Chevron responded by joining the Global Climate Coalition, a group that lobbied to convince politicians that more science on climate change was necessary before taking any action. Soon the United Nations became involved in studying climate change and attempting to bring the world together to slow it. In 1990, the U.N. International Panel on Climate Change issued its first report, which said the world was warming, and that even more future warming was likely. Two years later the United Nations held the Earth Summit in Rio de Janeiro in which tens of thou-

On March 24, 1989, the tanker *Exxon Valdez* ruptured its hull and spilled nearly 11 million gallons of its 53-million-allon cargo of crude oil in remote but scenic Prince William Sound, Alaska, making the *Exxon Valdez* the largest oil spill in U.S. waters. The environmental disaster severely affected wildlife, and its effects on Artic habitat has lasted far longer than scientists expected. The ship ran aground after trying to avoid icebergs.

sands of representatives from 172 countries participated in talks on how to slow global warming.

President George H. W. Bush attended the summit but rejected concrete targets to cut emissions. Instead he promised to return the country's emissions to 1990 levels by 2000. Increasing demand for fuels, including oil and coal—the burning of which emits more carbon dioxide than any other fossil fuel—made that goal impossible.

Hansen's testimony had given new life to the environmental movement that had taken root in the 1970s. But the U.S. addiction to oil was deepening and the country's carbon dioxide emissions were rising. While car makers had made big gains in making fuel-efficient cars, more autos were being sold. And many of them were of a new breed that did not have to comply with fuel standards.

Under financial pressure from imports of Japanese cars into the United States, Detroit automakers had lobbied to exempt light trucks from the CAFE standards that had been adopted in response to high oil prices in the 1970s. In the 1980s Chrysler avoided bankruptcy in part by producing the family minivan. An Environmental Protection Agency rule said vehicles would be exempt from the mileage standards if they were designed to carry property or were a "derivation of such a vehicle."

So Chrysler built the minivan on top of a truck platform. It was less costly to make than cars because it did not have to meet the mileage standards. It was less costly to buy because it escaped a tax on gas guzzlers.

In the 1990s, Chrysler again led the way by producing the sports utility vehicle (SUV). They picked a good moment for the debut; the economy was booming and gasoline prices were low. Ford and GM soon made SUVs which helped lead to the resurrection of the U.S. auto industry. SUVs were not much more difficult to produce than pickup trucks, but when tricked out with a few gadgets, such as a nice radio, they could fetch much higher prices. By 2000, two thirds of Detroit's sales and almost all of their profits came from SUVs, mini-vans, and pickups.

Americans' hunger for big, powerful SUVs eventually helped cut the average gas mileage of the country's vehicle fleet. The average efficiency of all cars and light trucks peaked at 25.9 miles per gallon in 1987 and 1988. But the craze for SUVs helped push that down to 24.5 mpg by 1997 and to 23.9 mpg by 2001. SUVs also helped push U.S. gasoline demand higher through the 1990s.

U.S. gasoline consumption of 7.2 million bpd in 1991 rose to 8 million bpd by 1997 and hit 9.1 million bpd in 2004, according to the Energy Information Administration.

After years of steadily growing world oil demand, OPEC officially decided in late 1997 at a meeting in Indonesia to raise output. In reality, the agreement was an endorsement of action by some of its members, like Venezuela, that had

already increased production in anticipation of growing global demand. The production boosts came also because of fears about the quick recovery of Iraqi oil output. Iraq was still a member of OPEC, but its official output was now controlled by the United Nations. Many OPEC producers like Saudi Arabia needed cash and did not want Iraq to gain a bigger piece of the global oil market.

But the production boosts could not have come at a worse time for OPEC. The Asian economic crisis had already rocked Thailand and was soon to spread to Indonesia and Korea. The 1998 winter was mild in the United States, Europe, and Japan, which cut demand for heating oil. In addition, Iraq more than doubled oil output.

Technology had responded somewhat to the growth in world oil demand. There was no new miracle motor fuel to replace oil, but advancements helped drillers get better at finding and removing oil from the crags and crevices of underground oil reservoirs. Producers were now using horizontal drilling as opposed to drilling straight down. Computer programs helped drillers analyze data from sound waves sent deep into the earth to form detailed pictures of reservoirs. They tapped old fields that had been long thought depleted, which lowered the overall costs of producing oil. Companies also invested heavily in offshore oil drilling in the Gulf of Mexico and off Angola in which new platforms could reach depths of a mile down or more.

As a result of the production boosts and faith in new oil sources, U.S. oil prices collapsed from seventeen dollars a barrel in late 1997 to less than ten dollars through February 1999. Some industry watchers thought oil prices would keep falling. A March 1999 cover story in the magazine the *Economist* suggested that prices could fall to five dollars a barrel.

In fact the opposite happened. OPEC skillfully engaged non-OPEC producers Mexico, Norway, and Russia to cut output and raise prices. A year later U.S. oil prices had jumped to nearly thirty dollars a barrel and OPEC was back in the driver's seat.

Still the idea of a new world of cheap oil persisted. Analysts in the journal *Foreign Affairs* wrote in the winter of 2000 that rising oil prices had led to worries about dwindling supplies. "The energy problem looming in the early 21st century is neither skyrocketing prices nor shortages that herald the beginning of the end of the oil age. Instead the danger is precisely the opposite; long-term trends point to a prolonged oil surplus and low oil prices over the next two decades." The surplus would linger not just from the easy availability of world oil supplies, it said, but from advancements in automobiles, like hybrid cars running on both a small engine run on gasoline and an electric motor charged when drivers hit the brakes.

As prices stayed high, the question of how to secure America's future oil played a big role in the 2000 presidential campaign between Vice President Al Gore and George W. Bush, the son of George H. W. Bush. Both candidates wanted to slow growing U.S. dependence on foreign oil. A leader of an OPEC nation close to home was causing a headache for Washington. President Hugo Chavez of Venezuela had been instrumental in organizing the OPEC production cuts earlier that year that raised global prices. He was friendly with Cuba's dictator Fidel Castro and Iraq's Saddam Hussein.

Gore focused on demand, asserting that conservation could tame America's growing

George W. Bush at a Texas oil field.
*(Courtesy of the George Bush Presidential Library)*

oil thirst. He favored building light rail systems in cities and development of new vehicles to run on batteries or hydrogen fuel cells. He opposed drilling in Alaska's Arctic National Wildlife Refuge, which he said would only supply about the amount of oil that the country burned in six months.

Bush, on the other hand, focused on securing supply of fossil fuels and saw oil development in the refuge as an appropriate step to fight growing dependence on foreign oil. Crude held at about thirty dollars a barrel in the autumn of 2000, levels which were considered by many to be unbearably high. It was a famously tight race, but in the end Bush became president.

Dick Cheney, who headed the oil services company Halliburton Inc. before becoming Bush's vice president, said in 2001, "Conservation may be a sign of personal virtue, but it is not a sufficient basis for a sound, comprehensive energy policy." Cheney formed a task force to shape federal energy policy. He was mostly interested in boosting the supply of fossil fuels. Oil and gas drilling in the Arctic refuge could spare wildlife because new technology could keep the affected area down to 2,000 acres or "one-fifth the size of Dulles Airport" in metropolitan Washington, D.C., he said.

After the suicide attacks by airline hijackers on New York's twin towers and on the Pentagon in Washington, the call for reducing dependence on foreign oil grew louder after the suicide attacks by airline hijackers on New York's twin towers and on the Pentagon near Washington. After all, Osama bin Laden, the founder of the al-Qaeda fundamentalist Muslim group who claimed responsibility for organizing the attacks, was originally from Saudi Arabia.

Soon after the attacks, Bush launched war against the Taliban in Afghanistan where bin Laden had been living and helping to recruit and train attackers. The United States failed to capture or kill bin Laden, who was thought to be hiding

A New York City fire fighter looks at the remains of one of the Twin Towers of the World Trade Center, destroyed on September 11, 2001, when Al-Qaeda terrorists crashed two commercial jet airliners into the buildings.

somewhere in the mountain caves between Afghanistan and Pakistan.

The administration tried hard to convince the American people that Saddam Hussein was linked with the September 11 attacks even though there was no proof. Bush accused Hussein of harboring weapons of mass destruction. "We have seen that those who hate America are willing to crash airplanes into buildings full of innocent people," Bush said in late 2002. "Our enemies would be no less willing, in fact, they would be eager, to use a biological, or chemical, or a nuclear weapon."

In 2003 Bush opened war against Iraq by dropping bombs on Baghdad. The weapons of mass destruction were not found. Instead of being greeted as liberators by the Iraqi people, as the administration had predicted, U.S. troops and contractors in Iraq were targets of militia armies. Fighting broke out between the Shiites and minority Sunnis who had held power during Hussein's reign.

Bush had said oil exports, which had never fully recovered from the 1990 Gulf War, would pay for reconstruction of the country. Before the 2003 invasion, Iraq's output had been near 2.5 million bpd. Afterwards, production ground to nearly a halt and only improved slowly despite the capture of Hussein. Militants bombed major oil pipelines. Three years after war started output was below 2 million bpd. "There is nothing in 2006 that makes us believe things will get better," said a former official at Iraq's oil ministry. "When we see killing, mayhem and the fragmentation, what is the significance of the oil industry?"

Other OPEC members like Saudi Arabia had boosted output to replace the lost Iraqi oil, but that was not enough to stop

Venezuelan protesters march to show their disapproval after their president, Hugo Chavez, fired workers from the state-run oil company, Petroleos de Venezuela. *(AP Images/Gregorio Marrero)*

Inset image: An oil refinery in Venezuela *(AP Images/Sincor/HO)* a price rally that started in 2002 and lasted six years. In 2003 strife in fellow OPEC members Venezuela, where a failed coup had tried to oust President Hugo Chavez, and in Nigeria, which was plagued with civil war, helped keep prices rising.

As the Iraq war dragged on, global economies boomed which increased demand. Despite rising petroleum prices, one of the biggest jumps in global oil demand ever came in 2004 when the world burned 82.4 million bpd of crude, a rise of 2.7 million bpd in one year.

Rising oil prices stirred a debate about exactly how much petroleum the world had left. One event shook those who believed cheap oil supplies would last far into the future. In early 2004 Shell Oil disclosed it had overstated its commercially producible oil reserves by nearly 4 billion barrels or 20 percent. That led to doubts about the reserve estimates of other producers. Soon U.S-based El Paso Corp cut its estimates of natural gas reserves by 41 percent.

If energy supplies were being revised by companies whose stocks traded in the United States, which was thought to have the world's toughest standards for reserve estimates, what, some wondered, might reserves be in parts of the world that were more secretive? Uncertainty about reserves in OPEC countries was greatest. The more oil an OPEC country claimed to have underground, the bigger a group quota it got and the more money it could generate in sales. Many believed that some OPEC countries fudged their numbers to get a bigger quota. "Without question, reserves reported for OPEC members don't fit the strict definitions of those reported by the U.S. or most European countries," said Bob Tippee, editor of the Oil & Gas Journal.

The debate got hotter after Houston banker Matthew Simmons questioned whether Saudi Arabia sat on top of as much oil as it claimed. He had visited the kingdom in 2003 and found high levels of water in output from the country's main oilfield, which he claimed meant it was in decline. His comments spurred Saudi Aramco to issue a rare breakdown of its petroleum resources that said the kingdom expected to add at least 150 billion barrels to the company's proven oil reserves by 2025.

In addition, a group of geologists and analysts who believed the world was swiftly running out of oil had come together in a movement called "peak oil." The group believed that the world's amount of oil available was at a peak or would peak in 2007, which would lead to disastrous consequences such as more wars and mass starvation. Their icon was the late M. King Hubbert, a geologist for Shell who said in 1956 that U.S. oil output would peak between the late 1960s and early 1970s. Most oilmen scoffed at Hubbert, but his prediction came true in 1970.

Simmons, a peak oil advocate, wrote a book in 2005 called *Twilight in the Desert*. He looked at scores of research papers published by geologists in Saudi Arabia and concluded that its five key oilfields were declining. In response to the book, the director of the Saudi Information Office in Washington said if the kingdom revealed any more of its geologic data it risked "giving terrorists a road map" to its most precious resource.

The year of 2007 passed and the world's oil supply did not peak. But it became clear that cheap oil supplies would be harder to find. In its 2008 annual forecast, the International Energy Agency said that by 2030 the world would have to rely more heavily on unconventional sources of oil, like the gooey tar sands of Western Canada and on OPEC members in the Middle East.

Both options could be troubling for consumers. It takes enormous amounts of energy to separate crude from the oil sands. The problem is so difficult that in the 1950s the U.S. Atomic Energy Commission prepared to supply an atomic bomb to test a theory that an underground blast could do the work relatively cheaply—until it was realized that the oil would be radioactive. So oil companies do the work with natural gas, which is not only costly and raises the price of the oil, but also releases enormous amounts of greenhouse gas.

And since OPEC countries have most of the world's remaining oil reserves, the continued reliance on petroleum would likely increase tensions between the Middle East and consumers. U.S. fuel demand fell after oil hit $147 in 2008, which helped push down prices. But demand was growing from a new part of the world. Early in the new century Asia became the world's top region for growth in oil demand. A race is already on for oil from the Middle East and North Africa because China and India, which want to industrialize like the United States has, have little oil of their own.

In 2000, China had 16 million cars; just four years later it had 27 million. That was still a small amount of cars compared to the United States, which with about a quarter of China's population of more than 1 billion people, had about 231 million cars in 2003. And China won't outpace the United States in total car ownership until sometime around 2030, according to estimates.

Still, China's thirst for new sources of oil is so great it has led in some cases to political embarrassment. For instance, China imports oil from Sudan, where it is also an investor and arms supplier. Human rights groups say China has done little to help stop bloodshed in Sudan's Darfur region, where the Sudanese army and government-backed Arab militias known as janjaweed have been fighting rebels, leaving about 200,000 dead and more than 2 million displaced. For its part, China says its investments bring development and benefits to the people of Sudan.

In the United States one indication that cheap oil supplies are becoming harder to find is the continued development of ultra deep oil drilling in the Gulf of Mexico—such as the long delayed Thunder Horse platform—despite the rise of hurricanes. Shell, for example, is developing Perdido, which at only eight miles from the maritime border with Mexico, has already stirred concerns within that country that the United States would be siphoning off some of its oil resources. And slowly but surely, countries bordering the Arctic, such as Russia and the United States, are exploring the polar region for oil riches. Some 25 percent of world's undiscovered oil and natural gas lies in the Arctic, the U.S. Geological Survey estimates. The petroleum is expensive to produce and ship to market, but unless the world cuts demand, it may become the next frontier.

The good news is many solutions to the oil crunch could come from the newest consumers. China, for instance, is a leader in electric motorbikes and scooters. The lessons learned from the scooters could eventually help China make reliable electric cars, which many studies say are more efficient than cars that run on gasoline. Still, in China those cars would likely run on electricity that was generated by coal. They could become cleaner if businesses found an economical way to store greenhouse gas emissions from coal-fired power plants permanently underground, or if the country got more of its power from low emissions sources like nuclear or wind and solar power.

China is also making advances in public transportation, particularly with rapid buses that are beginning to rush down special lanes on many of its highways and operate much like subways in other cities around the world. China's leadership could have lessons for other countries.

In America, there is also a sense that people are becoming more serious about the problem. President Barack Obama directed the federal government in his second week of his administration to speed up efforts by states and U.S. agencies to make cars get better mileage, becoming the first U.S. president to push for action when oil prices were nowhere near record prices. China and the United States and all other consumers will have to work together, because as the world's population is expected to hit about 9 billion people by about 2050 the supply of cheap oil is not growing. Indeed, it is vanishing fast.

# The Power of Wind

Billionaire Texas oil executive T. Boone Pickens wants wind power to drastically cut the amount of gasoline burned in U.S. cars. Actually his idea has two steps. First, build fleets of wind farms in the gustiest parts of the country, especially in a central strip of the country from Mexico to Canada, to generate electricity that would free up the natural gas burned for that purpose. Then burn the natural gas in cars, instead of gasoline, which can cut emissions of the greenhouse gas carbon dioxide by 30 percent. To kick the plan off, he's hoping to one day build one of the world's largest wind farms in Texas and investing in a company that converts cars to run on natural gas. He says the plan would slash the country's dependence on oil imports, saving Americans hundreds of billions of dollars per year.

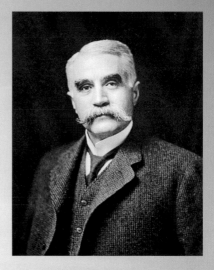

Whether or not Pickens fully succeeds in changing the way Americans use energy is unclear. But his plan is a symbol of how far wind power, one of the oldest sources of energy humans have harnessed, has come. The Persians built windmills as early as 1000 BC for grinding grains and the technology spread to the Roman Empire. By the nineteenth century, tens of thousands of windmills across Europe crushed wheat and pumped water.

Inventor Charles Brush (top photo). Brush built this 60-foot, 80,000-pound wind turbine in 1887, making it the world's first automatically operated wind turbine.

The Ohio inventor Charles Brush built what is thought to have been the first wind turbine to generate power in 1887. It was a monster compared to today's sleek turbines with 144 blades, and it only generated a small amount of electricity. By the 1930s many U.S. farmers used far simpler turbines to power their lights because the electric grid hadn't reached them yet. Then after the oil shocks of the 1970s, California built some of the world's first wind farms filled with fifty-five kilowatt turbines. But once the oil price fell in the 1980s, politicians cut the subsidies and few new farms sprouted.

Meanwhile the Danish wind industry had taken off after World War II cut off the country's oil shipments. Now the country gets 20 percent of its power from wind and Vestas is the largest wind power company in the world.

Worries about recent record fuel costs and carbon dioxide emissions have led to a global wind power renaissance. In the United States, installment of wind power turbines grew by about 50 percent in 2008 and that year the country surpassed Germany to become the world's largest generator of wind power. And today's turbines are 550 kilowatts, or ten times the size of the ones from the 1970s and 1980s. New ones being built are 1.5 megawatts, and in Germany a 4 Mw prototype wind turbine is running.

Still the United States only gets about 1 percent of its power from the wind and increasing that to a more significant portion will take a great deal more than just putting up turbines. The electric power grid is antiquated. Conceived of more than one hundred years ago, the grid on which power is transmitted from power plants to consumers typing at computers or basking in air conditioning, resembles a network of small country lanes.

In fact, new wind power centers such as the Maple Ridge Wind farm in upstate New York have had to occasionally shut down as wind generation grows faster than new transmission. A new superhighway of transmission lines is needed to realize the potential of the renewable energy. And that opens up a host of problems, especially in the United States where people concerned about development coined the phrase NIMBY, or "not in my backyard." Building new transmission lines in ecologically sensitive regions such as national and state parks could pit conservationists against wind power advocates.

Pickens himself admits that the federal government would have to become much more involved to build a superhighway of high-voltage transmission lines. In some cases the government might have to use the power of eminent domain, or seizing of private property for the public good, to get access to space for building new power lines. The problem is that new transmission projects have almost always occurred at state and local levels, while a national plan would take much more forethought. It would also take money—up to $60 billion, though it wouldn't have to be spent all at once.

The good thing is that once the wind turbines and power lines are up and paid for, the energy generated is free, meaning any long term planning could have a major payoff. ■

# Biofuels: The Next Generation

The Pentagon's research arm wants to know if the future of fuel lurks in pond scum. As the world's top buyer of fuel, the U.S. military is eager to move past volatile oil prices as much as it can and ensure secure access to energy in the future. So the Defense Advanced Research Projects Agency (DARPA) recently awarded contracts worth tens of millions of dollars to companies that are seeking to slash the costs of making biodiesel from algae—one of the planet's oldest life forms.

The Pentagon's interest is a sign of not only the wisdom of beginning to look beyond petroleum, but also of the limitations of today's biofuels. Algae have advantages over traditional biofuels, like ethanol made from corn, or biodiesel made from soybean oil. Algae basically need only water, sunshine, and carbon dioxide to grow. That means farming algae, or algaculture, would less likely be blamed for helping to raise food prices than the corn ethanol and soy biodiesel industries have been. In addition, algae can produce far more fuel per acre than corn or soy and it can be grown in containers filled with fresh, salt, or waste water.

Algae fuel is just one of the so-called next generation biofuels that have promise but are not yet commercially available. They are still more costly to produce than gasoline, but developments in research are pushing the price down.

Biofuels, in particular ethanol, have been around for nearly as long as cars.

Henry Ford's famous Model T cars were made to run on gasoline or ethanol made from grains, or a blend of both. Gasoline won the early fuel race because it was easier to drill crude and process it in refineries than to grow plants, convert their starches into sugars, and distill that into fuel.

But during oil price shocks of the 1970s, a renewed interest in biofuels took root. For a short while the Department of Energy funded research into algal fuels known as the Aquatic Species Program. Then the U.S. Congress took the first of many steps to promote corn ethanol as an alternative fuel. It seemed like a good solution that could reduce dependence on foreign oil while giving farmers a whole new market to sell to.

As oil prices rallied for six years after 2002 on growing global demand, the U.S. government boosted incentives and mandates for making corn ethanol, and distilleries sprouted up all over the country, particularly in the Midwest. But as oil prices soared, corn prices also rose as grains were now thought of not only as a source of food, but as fuel. There were many other factors besides the soaring ethanol industry for rising food prices, but the issue left ethanol with a black eye.

Another problem with corn-based ethanol is uncertainty about whether the amount of energy put into growing corn

and making it into fuel is greater than the amount of energy that comes from burning the finished ethanol product. The ethanol industry points to studies that say newfound efficiencies in the way distilleries are run and corn is harvested make it a clear winner. But doubts remain.

As a result, many new companies, and even traditional ethanol companies like South Dakota-based Poet, the largest ethanol distiller in the world, are focusing on beginning to make ethanol from nonfood crops or plant waste, like corn cobs. The new fuel is called cellulosic ethanol because it can be made from breaking down the tough woody bits of plants, called cellulose, into fuel.

"The fuel of the future," Ford told the Associated Press in 1925, "is going to come from . . . apples, weeds, sawdust— almost anything." The main thing standing in the way of this vision is cost. Distillers need to break down the cellulose with one of several industrial processes that are not perfected yet. One uses substances such as enzymes

from fungi that eat through canvas tents in the sweltering jungle to attack cellulose, another rips it apart with the help of large amounts of heat and pressure, such as an oil refinery uses to break down crude. The extra costs have kept next-generation biofuels out of reach.

Algae-based biodiesel also has hurdles. For one thing it's difficult to grow a desired strain of algae without countless other undesirable strains of the organism mucking up the batch. Also, until new methods improve the process, it takes a lot of energy to dry the algae and press it to remove the oil. What gives producers hope for algae and other next-generation biofuels is that the industry is young, especially compared with the oil business. ■

# Timeline

### 3000 BC
Oil seeping to the surface in Mesopotamia tapped for building mortar.

### 1848
Samuel Kier packages oil from salt wells near Pittsburgh for sale as patent medicine.

### 1859
"Colonel" Edwin Drake drills the first prolific U.S. oil well in Pennsylvania inspiring the first petroleum rush; the oil is burned in lamps, wiping out the whale oil business.

### 1879
Thomas Edison invents the incandescent light bulb, threatening the growing petroleum business.

### 1896
Henry Ford builds gasoline-burning "Quadricycle," a prototype of the modern mass-produced sedan.

### 1901
On a Texas hill called Spindletop, drillers strike gusher that produces more than all the other wells on the planet combined.

### 1912
Winston Churchill begins to convert the British Navy from coal to oil.

### 1913
More than 1 million cars and trucks chug across America and Europe, most running on petroleum fuels.

### 1956

Shell Oil consultant M. King Hubbert predicts U.S. oil production will peak; U.S. President Eisenhower pushes through Interstate Highway System.

### 1960

Group of oil producing nations form the Organization of the Petroleum Exporting Countries in Baghdad (OPEC) to control oil prices.

### 1970

U.S. oil production peaks.

### 1973

Yom Kippur War results in Arab oil embargo, the first global oil shock.

### 1975

Automobile efficiency standards established in the United States.

### 1977

U.S. President Jimmy Carter says balancing energy demands with domestic resources is the "the moral equivalent of war."

### 1979

The Iranian revolution that topples the Shah leads to second global oil shock.

### 1991

First Gulf War.

### 1997

OPEC miscalculates by boosting oil production ahead of the Asian economic crisis; oil drops to eleven dollars a barrel.

### 2001

Toyota starts selling the Prius hybrid globally.

### 2003

U.S. invades Iraq, second Gulf War starts.

## 2005

Hurricanes Katrina and Rita shut down U.S. oil and natural gas production in the Gulf of Mexico.

## 2008

In July, oil hits record $147 a barrel on global demand; U.S. drivers cut demand sharply;U.S. Geological Survey says a quarter of world's undiscovered oil lies in the Arctic.

## 2009

Barack Obama becomes first U.S. president to call for strict conservation measures at a time when oil is far below record price.

# Sources

## Chapter One: The Gathering Storm

p. 12, "Hurricanes season is one . . ." Timothy Gardner, "Hurricanes Threaten Growth in Offshore Oil," *Houston Chronicle*, August 7, 2005.

## Chapter Two: Pennsylvania Hills

p. 21, "Take out what you've got . . ." John Moody, *The Masters of Capital: A Chronicle of Wall Street.* (New Haven: Yale University Press, 1921), 53.

p. 22, "Every day is 'Independence Day . . ." Steven Watts, *The People's Tycoon: Henry Ford and the American Century* (New York: Alfred A. Knopf, 2005), 127.

p. 24, "the oldest man . . . " Ida Tarbell, *All in the Day's Work* (Boston: G. K. Hall, 1985), 235-236.

## Chapter Three: Ruling the Seas

p. 34, "weren't a darn . . ." Rachel Bronson, *Thicker than Oil: America's Uneasy Partnership with Saudi Arabia* (Oxford: Oxford University Press, 2006), 55.

## Chapter Four: Boom Time to Growth Limits

p. 41, "Texas oil fields have been . . ." Daniel Yergin, *The Prize: The Epic Quest for Oil, Money and Power* (New York: Simon & Schuster, 1991), 567.

p. 42, "big hard blow . . ." Yergin, *The Prize*, 585.

p. 43, "His majesty is calling wolf . . ." Douglas Little, *American Orientalism: The United State and the Middle East Since 1945* (Chapel Hill: The University of North Carolina Press, 2002), 68.

p. 46, "the pumps were barricaded . . ." Lawrence Fellows, "Harried 'Gas' Dealers Try Barricades," *New York Times*, December 28, 1973.

p. 46    "This winter, when there . . ." Edward Cowan,
         "Saudi Oil Terms for U.S. Outlined," *New York Times*,
         November 6, 1973.

p. 47,   "This year we will drive . . ." Richard Nixon,
         "Remarks at the Lighting of the Nations Christmas Tree,"
         December 14, 1973, http://www.presidency.ucsb.edu/ws/index.
         php?pid=4072.

p. 48,   "The United States . . . " Yergin, *The Prize,* 616.

p. 51,   "the moral equivalent . . ." Jimmy Carter, "The president's
         Proposed Energy Policy," (televised speech April 18, 1977),
         http://www.pbs.org/wgbh/amex/carter/filmmore/ps_energy.html.

p. 53,   "position as the international . . ." Bronson, *Thicker
         Than Oil*, 146.

p. 56,   "Two of our members . . ." William Borders,
         "OPEC's Iraq Parley Called Off," *New York Times*,
         October 9, 1980.

p. 56,   "The oil weapon . . ." Barbara Slavin, "The World:
         OPEC Agrees to Limits on Production," *New York
         Times*, March 21, 1982.

p. 61,   "People are starting to say . . ." Peter Applebome,
         "Climbing Oil Prices Bring Sigh of Relief to
         Southwest, but Edginess Remains," *New York Times*, July 23, 1987

p. 64,   "partly for a lark . . ." Tom Lewis, *Divided
         Highways* (New York, NY: Viking Penguin, 1991), 90.

p. 64,   "we were not sure . . ." David A. Pfeiffer, "Ike's
         Interstate at 50," *Prologue* 38, no. 2 (Summer 2006), http//
         www.archives.gov/publications/prologue/2006/summer/
         interstates.html.

p. 65,   "through darkest America . . ." Lewis, *Divided Highways*, 90.

p. 65,   "thinking about good . . ." Ibid.

p. 65,   "I decided . . ." Ibid, 91.

p. 69,   "We cannot fail," Nao Nakanishi and Niu Shuping,
         "China Builds Plant to Turn Coal into Barrels of Oil,"
         Reuters, June 4, 2008.

# Chapter Five: What's Left?

p. 71,   "Iraqis will not forget . . ." Youssef Ibrahim, "Iraq
         Threatens Emirates and Kuwait on Oil Glut,"
         *New York Times*, July 18, 1990.

p. 75,   "99 percent confidence," James Hansen, testimony
         to U.S. Senate Energy and Natural Resources
         Committee, June 23, 1988,
         http://www.audubonmagazine.org/global.html.

p. 78, "derivation of such a vehicle . . ." Daniel Sperling
and Deborah Gordon, *Two Billion Cars: Driving Toward Sustainability* (Oxford: Oxford University Press, 2009), 53.

p. 81, "The energy problem . . ." Amy Myers Jaffe and
Robert A. Manning, "The Shocks of a World of
Cheap Oil," *Foreign Affairs*, January/February 2000.

p. 82, "Conservation may be a sign . . ." Dick Cheney,
interview by Jim Lehrer, *MacNeil/Lehrer
NewsHour*, PBS, July 18, 2001,
http://www.pbs.org/newshour/bb/white_house/july-dec01/
cheney_7-18.html.

p. 82, "one-fifth the size of Dulles Airport . . ." Joseph
Kahn, "Cheney Promotes Increasing Supply as Energy Policy,"
*New York Times*, May 1, 2001.

p. 84, "We have seen . . ." George W.
Bush, "Bush: don't Wait for Mushroom Cloud,"
(transcript of televised speech on October 8, 2002),
http://archives.cnn.com/2002/ALLPOLITICS/10/07/bush.transcript/.

p. 84, "There is nothing in . . ." Ghaida Ghantous and
Mariam Karouny, "Rapid Recovery in Iraq Oil
Sector Unlikely," Reuters, March 16, 2006.

p. 86, "Without question . . . Barbara Lewis, "Murky
OPEC Data Muddies Oil Reserves Debate," Reuters, April 5, 2004.

p. 87, "giving terrorists . . ." Timothy Gardner and Chris
Baltimore, "Saudi Geologists' Papers Spell Lower
Output –Book," Reuters, May 27, 2005.

p. 98, "The fuel of the future . . ." "Ford Predicts Fuel from
Vegetation," *New York Times*, September 20, 1925.

# Bibliography

## Books

Bradsher, Keith. *High and Mighty: The World's Most Dangerous Vehicles and How they Got that Way.* New York: Public Affairs, 2002.

Bronson, Rachel. *Thicker than Oil: America's Uneasy Partnership with Saudi Arabia.* Oxford: Oxford University Press, 2006.

Carson, Iain, and Vijay V. Vaitheeswaran. Zoom: *The Global Race to Power the Car of the Future.* New York: Twelve, 2007.

Giddens, Paul H. *The Birth of the Oil Industry.* New York: The,MacMillan Company, 1938.

Little, Douglas. *American Orientalism: The United States and the Middle East Since 1945.* Chapel Hill: The University of North Carolina Press, 2002.

Marcel, Valerie, and John V. Mitchell. *Oil Titans: Oil Companies in the Middle East.* London: Royal Institute of International Affairs, 2006

Margonelli, Lisa. *Oil on the Brain: Adventures from the Pump to the Pipeline.* New York: Doubleday, 2007.

Moody, John. *The Masters of Capital: A Chronicle of Wall Street.* New Haven: Yale University Press, 1921.

Patterson, James, T. *Grand Expectations: The United States,* 1945-1974. Oxford: Oxford University Press, 1996.

Sperling, Daniel, and Deborah Gordon. *Two Billion Cars: Driving Toward Sustainability.* Oxford: Oxford University Press, 2009

Watts, Steven. *The People's Tycoon: Henry Ford and the American Century.* New York: Alfred A. Knopf, 2005.

Yergin, Daniel. *The Prize: The Epic Quest for Oil, Money and Power.* New York: Simon and Schuster, 1991.

## Periodicals

Applebome, Peter. "Climbing Oil Prices Bring Sigh of Relief to Southwest, but Edginess Remains." *New York Times*, July 23, 1987.

Borders, William. "OPEC's Iraq Parley Called Off." *New York Times*, October 9, 1980.

Cowan, Edward. "Saudi Oil Terms for U.S. Outlined." *New York Times*, November 6, 1973.

Fellows, Lawrence. "Harried 'Gas' Dealers Try Barricades." *New York Times*, December 28, 1973.

"Ford Predicts Fuel from Vegetation." *New York Times*, September 20, 1925.

Gardner, Timothy. "Hurricanes Threaten Growth in Offshore Oil." *Houston Chronicle*, August 7, 2005.

Gardner, Timothy, and Chris Baltimore. "Saudi Geologists' Papers Spell Lower Output – Book." Reuters, May 27, 2005.

Ghaida Ghantous, and Mariam Karouny, "Rapid Recovery in Iraq Oil Sector Unlikely." Reuters, March 16, 2006.

Ibrahim, Youssef. "Iraq threatens Emirates and Kuwait on Oil Glut." *New York Times*, July 18, 1990.

Jaffe, Amy, Myers, and Manning, Robert, A. "The Shocks of a World of Cheap Oil." *Foreign Affairs*. January/February 2000.

Kolbert, Elizabeth. "Unconventional Crude." *New Yorker*, November 12, 2007.

Lewis, Barbara. "Murky OPEC Data Muddies Oil Reserves Debate." Reuters, April 5, 2004.

Nao Nakanishi, and Niu Shuping, "China Builds Plant to turn Coal into Barrels of Oil." Reuters, June 4, 2008.

Revkin, Andrew C. "Endless Summer – Living with the Greenhouse Effect." *Discover*, October, 1988.

Slavin, Barbara. "The World; OPEC Agrees to Limits on Production." *New York Times*, March 21, 1982.

Wald, Matthew, L. "Wind Energy Bumps into Power Grid's Limits." *New York Times*, August, 27, 2008.

# Web sites

**U.S. Energy Information Administration**
http://www.eia.doe.gov

**International Energy Agency**
http://www.iea.org

**Organization of the Petroleum Exporting Countries**
http://www.opec.org

**BP Statistical Review of World Energy**
http://www.bp.com/productlanding.do?categoryId=6929&contentId=7044622

**The Oil Depletion Analysis Centre**
http://www.odac-info.org/

**The Oil Drum: Discussions about Energy and Our Future**
http://www.theoildrum.com/

# Index

# M

Middle East oil production, 27–28, 30, 42
Mobil, 25, 34, 49
Mossadegh, Mohammed, 35–36
Muslims, 53, 55, 82

# N

National Iranian Oil Company, 49
nationalization of oil production, 35, 48–49
Nixon, Richard, 43–44, 47

# O

Obama, Barack, 90–91
offshore drilling, 11, 47, 51, 80
oil reserves, 30, 43, 48, 73, 86–87
oil well, early, *18–19*
oil, early years of development, 15–17, 20–22, 24–25
OPEC, 39, 48, 49, 55–56, 79–80
Operation Desert Storm, *73*

# P

peak oil, 86–87
Pearl Harbor, 30, *32*, 33
*Perdido* (oil platform), 89
Pickens, T. Boone, 92–93, 95
prices of oil, 38–39, 44–45, 60–61
Prince William Sound, *76–77*, 77

# Q

Qaddafi, Muammar al-, 42

# R

Reagan, Ronald, 60, 61
Rockefeller, John D., 20, 21, *21*, 22, 24, 30
Roosevelt, Franklin D., 32, 33, 65
Roosevelt, Kermit, 35–36, *35*

# S

Sasol, 67, 68, *68*
Saudi Arabia, 43, 55, 56, 58–59, 86
September 11, 82, *83*, 84
Shah of Iran, 44, 49, 51, 52, 53
Shell Oil, 24, 51, 86, 87, 89
Simmons, Matthew, 86, 87
Six Day War, 39
*Spindletop* (oil platform), 22–23
Standard Oil, 21, 22, 24, 30, 33
Strategic Petroleum Reserve, 48, 51
synthetic fuel production, 32, 68

# T

Texaco, 24, 49
Texas Oil Company, 33
*Thunder Horse* (oil platform), 11, *13*, 89
Trans Alaskan Pipeline, 49–50, *49*, 71
Trans-Arabian Pipeline, 34
turbines, wind, 93–94, *93*

# U

U.S. Geological Survey, 89

# W

wind power, 92–93, 95

# Y

Yamani, Sheikh, 42, 43, 46, 49, 60
Yom Kippur War, 43